Resumes for Children
17 Years Old and Under

Yes Really!

by

Donna Kristine Manley

Copyright © 2005 by Donna Kristine Manley

Resumes for Children
17 Years Old and Under
by Donna Kristine Manley

Cover Design by Vita Rome

Editor: Beryle Manley

Printed in the United States of America

ISBN - 10: 0-9777835-0-2
ISBN - 13: 978-0-9777835-0-2

Library of Congress Control Number: 2006900511

DISCLAIMER

Names, addresses, e-mail addresses, phone and/or facsimile numbers, some software names, some names of businesses and organizations, the sample references and cover letters used in this book, are fictitious and do NOT reflect personal knowledge of actual individuals, educational institutions, businesses, resources, or locales by the author, editor, publisher, distributor(s), or any other people with whom they have to do. Any resemblance to people living or dead, places, or things that exist or are defunct, are purely coincidental.

END OF DISCLAIMER

Published by:
Christiana Press, LLC
P.O. Box 81428
Conyers, GA 30013
http://www.resumesforchildren.com

TABLE OF CONTENTS

DEDICATION

✦

This book is dedicated to _____, to all children, and your nurturers everywhere. As you grow we will help safeguard your future by giving you the tools you need to succeed. May this book bring you rich ideas, inspiration, and hope. May it bring forth your creative "juices." May your thoughts and dreams come to reality, and fulfill your deepest expectations.

Kris

"Acquire Wisdom! Acquire Understanding!"

INTRODUCTION

※

As the gap widens between those who have and those who have not, it is important for our children to have advantages. Our children need to be those who have rather than those who have not. In order for them to be those who have, preparation must take place. Parents are encouraged to begin this preparation early in the child's life. Proud parents trumpet children's accomplishments, but trumpeting is not enough. Parents need to use their children's accomplishments, activities, skills, abilities, challenges, interests, and talents to propel them into becoming successful individuals. Extracurricular activities (activities outside the classroom) play a vital role in a child's future. Free time is fun and can be used wisely. What a child does with some of his or her free time can cost them in the future. Begin to build a child's future with their free time by filling some of it with worthwhile activities and opportunities to learn something new.

Parents can boost their children's self-esteem by taking the time to capture their accomplishments, activities, gifts, talents, and interests on paper. Create a resume / CAB (Child Activity Brief) for and with your child. Your child will certainly feel good about himself or herself. View your child's resume as exposing the treasure hidden inside him or her. As you and your child sit down together to construct this record it becomes a time of bonding.

It is a good thing for parents to persuade their children to strive for academic excellence. Of equal importance is how well rounded or balanced a child is outside the academic arena. It is good to have a list of references that include teachers, coaches, clergy, family, friends, community service organizations, and employment (if applicable). Please emphasize the importance of character references. If someone tells your child what a great job he or she has done or is doing ask for that person's appreciation in writing or in an e-mail. These serve as "feathers" in your child's "hat." If your child is age appropriate, sit down with him or her and go over the components of a job application. Review what questions are appropriate for prospective employers to ask during a job interview. Check with your Department of Labor. I'd be willing to bet some children wonder how Dad and Mom got their jobs. Children are very bright, do not underestimate them. Explain to your child what a resume is. Expose him or her to resume writing software, along with books that teach resume writing. Don't think it strange that colleges and universities may ask for resumes to accompany applications for entrance. A resume is a living document and can be revised. Teach your child that what should increase are NOT how many jobs one has had, but one's KSAs (Knowledge, Skills, and Abilities), gifts, talents, and accomplishments. Please keep one thing in mind, you DO NOT have to have a job to create a resume as you will see from the sample resumes in this book.

Children should be taught to leave an organization better than it was before they arrived. I was with a company for two years and before I arrived one of the company's manufacturing facilities maintained a food safety audit score of "Excellent." I prepared the facility for its second food safety audit by creating documents the facility didn't have but were vital. As a result, their score rose from "Excellent" to "Superior," the highest score possible. The third audit yielded the same score, a "Superior." I was later laid off by that company and was asked by my manager to send him, on CD (compact disc), all documentation I had developed. The company had the necessary documentation for future audits and was very pleased with my accomplishments. I added this to my resume.

The information contained in this book will give parents, guardians, and other nurturers a boost in assisting children on a road to successful and fruitful lives. In addition, this book will supplement, amplify, and complement other ideas you, the reader, may have. I urge you to tap into all sources and information and tailor them to your child's individual needs. Your child's resume will boost his or her morale by painting a clear picture of just how capable he or she is. Notably missing are objectives within most of the resumes; remember, we are dealing with children and most, like some adults, have not made a decision about a possible lifetime career.

This book contains sample resumes for children ages 17 years old and under, along with sample references and cover letters. You might ask yourself, why would a child need a resume? Consider the following:

— How impressive it will be when you submit your child's application to a special program, private school, a competition or event, and include his or her resume with the application.

— You may also use the resume to seek sponsorship from friends, family, and organizations in order for your child to gain admission to a program. Having such a document can validate your child's abilities.

— Use your child's resume to assist in seeking scholarships and grants.

— If your child were asked to tell something about himself or herself having a resume will help in answering that question.

In the back of this book are worksheets that you can use to record your reflections, ideas, and resources. In other words, carefully recall, reflect on, and write down what your child has done and is doing as they grow and learn about themselves and their world. Ask yourself what you can do to better your child's education. Seek out resources that are available to help your child make good choices and decisions.

Take this journey with me and look at some components of a resume for a child. We will explore the possibilities for different ages and situations. Consider the bulleted points below, but don't limit your options.

- Acting
- Arts, The
- Awards
- Bilingual Abilities
- Business Venture
- Camps
- Career Day
- Charitable Donations
- Clubs and other Organizations
- College Prep Programs
- Corporate Programs
- Dance
- Education
- Employment
- Financial Savvy
- Hobbies
- "Home" Training
- Honorable Mentions

- Internships / Fellowships
- Life's Challenges / Health Status
- Local or Global Service Initiatives
- Modeling
- Musical Abilities
- Newspaper Articles / Feature Stories
- Patents
- Radio Talk Shows
- Science & Technology Fair Participant
- Speaking Appearances
- Sports
- Student Council
- Student Tour Guide
- Summer Enrichment / Learning Series
- Television Appearances
- Training
- Travel, including international
- Youth Council Member

It's good to BE

YOUR OWN boss

ALL the time.

SAMPLE RESUME — <u>Entrepreneur and Volunteer</u>

Daniel Patel, age 15   2341 Cambridge Creek Circle
Phone: 294.000.0111   Westminster, Maryland 12345
Fax: 294.000.0101   E-mail: danielpatel777@_____.com

BUSINESS AND REVENUE INCREASE — May 2004 to Present
Listed business, **The Yard Jockey,** in subdivision's homeowners' association directory. During the summer months mow and maintain neighbors' yards, trim hedges, rake leaves, wash and vacuum vehicles, and sweep and remove cobwebs in garages. During the winter months shovel snow and salt driveways. Communicate notice of work availability to neighbors through e-mail.
Number of customers has doubled.

ENTREPRENUER DAY CAMP FOR YOUTH — I took the following weekend workshops:
January 2004 to March 2004
- Business Plan Development
- Managing Tasks
- Negotiating

- Phases of a Business Start-up
- Practical Goal Setting
- Setting up a Record-keeping System

VOLUNTEER
- Part of The Book Beat at local area hospital where, for one hour twice a week, I read books, letters, and cards to children being cared for on the cancer ward. September 2003 to Present
- Participant in Walk for the Fight Against Breast Cancer. Every April since 2001
- Co-chair for high school chapter of World Relief Organization — Current
- Chosen by World Relief Organization as one of ten high school students to work in Gabon (Africa) for two weeks: assisted in fishing for the village, helped build a house, and retrieved water for the village. This was a great experience! June 2005

French is the official language in Gabon, so with my being fluent in French I proved to be an asset to the organization by serving as an interpreter.

EDUCATION
School Name and Address

ORGANIZATIONS
National Scholar Society

ACTIVITIES
Enjoy playing chess and video games

SOFTWARE AND OPERATING SYSTEMS
Vitalectra (financial software), QuickBooks, Microsoft Word, Excel, PowerPoint, Access, Windows XP, Windows 2000, and Linux

AWARDS — November 2004
Received *The Business Excellence* award along with a profile in high school newspaper.

TRAVEL
Spent summer of 1998 with family in France where I began to learn French. Continued to take classes in French when we returned to the States.

TAKE *your*

SUCCESS AS

far as you can.

SAMPLE RESUME — Aspiring Pilot

Marisol Perez, age 16
Phone: 334.222.1171
Fax: 234.000.1712

1234 Sugar Creek Circle
Commodore, Virginia 12435
E-mail: Marisolswings@_____.com

Will gain admission to a professional flight program through an accredited university and obtain a degree in Aeronautical Engineering and Technology with Professional Flight concentration.

EDUCATION
School Name and Address
Anticipate graduating with Advanced College Preparatory Diploma and am part of a dual enrollment program in which I take college courses.
- Flight school student: Fly Cessna aircraft; to date logged 40 hours of flying time.
- I look forward to passing the private pilot written exam which is one of the first steps in obtaining my Private Pilot License. September 2004 to Present

AVIATION CAMP, Appleton, Virginia
Classroom instruction covered principles of flight, aviation and aerospace fundamentals, airplane engines, flight planning, navigation, and the air traffic control system. June 2003

CERTIFICATIONS AND LICENSES
Student Pilot License
Federal Aviation Administration (FAA) 3rd Class Medical Certificate
Child and Adult CPR (Cardiopulmonary Resuscitation) / Automated External Defibrillator (AED)

CAREER DAY SPEAKER
Visit high schools and elementary schools during the year to encourage students to pursue different career paths. Share my pursuit of being a pilot and letting kids know that you are never too young to begin living your dreams. January 2005 to Present

VOLUNTEER
- Mercy Medical Center, Commodore, Virginia —Assist in setting up equipment for blood drives one Saturday every other month for four hours. June 2004 to Present

NEW PROGRAM IMPLEMENTED
My program idea for our school to have a foreign language movie of the month was implemented September 2003 and is still going strong. The movies of course have English subtitles.

COMPUTER SOFTWARE AND OPERATING SYSTEMS
FlightSphere (Flight Simulation software), FlowRinga (flowchart software), Microsoft Word, Outlook Excel, PowerPoint, Access, Windows XP, Windows 2000, and Unix

ORGANIZATIONS	The Eagles' Society and National Scholar Society
HOBBIES	Gardening
MUSICAL INSTRUMENTS	Since I was seven years old have enjoyed playing the guitar.
LANGUAGES	Read, write, and speak Spanish

.

Art from the Heart

Nathaniel Smart, age 9

956 Chestnut Creek Drive
Hamlet Cove, New Mexico 54321
Phone: 334.700.0179
E-mail: nathanielsart@_____.com

INCOME GENERATED FROM HOBBY — April 2004 to Present

Create silhouettes from headshots of family members. I brought portfolio to class for Show & Tell. Many parents ask me to create headshot silhouettes of their children. Created and maintain an e-mail base of my growing list of customers. Christmas is one of my busiest times. I learned that grandparents love getting silhouettes of their grandchildren.

In July 2004 successfully held a home art exhibit featuring charcoal pencil drawings. Asked by neighbors to create and distribute catalog within the subdivision. The catalog was created and distributed through e-mail. Listed hobby in subdivision's homeowners' association directory.

CREATIVE SALES — Since June 2004

Participate in and have won several children's art contests. Set up a booth at local annual Children's Fall Festival where I sell my art. Suggest that parents display the art in a playroom or in a nursery.

TEACHER'S ASSISTANT — September 2004 to Present

This task is rotated among students. Responsibilities include: cleaning chalkboard, straightening bookshelves, dusting, turning off classroom computers, and shelving books in the school library.

CHARITABLE DONATIONS

Donated several colorful drawings to local children's hospital. My drawings hang in the main corridor just outside the children's ward.

INCREASED EXPOSURE

My drawings are displayed in these shops within our city square: Red's Café, Sophie's Eatery, and Kids' Kraze Clothing

SOFTWARE AND OPERATING SYSTEMS

PenSulare (image editing software), Microsoft Word, PowerPoint, Windows 2000, Windows XP, Mac OS9, and Mac OSX

OTHER INTERESTS

Enjoy playing video games, going to the Center for Puppetry Arts, and finding books on histories of art styles and techniques. I enjoy studying the paintings of famous American Artists like Georgia O'Keeffe and Frederic Remington, along with the paintings of French Artist, Claude Oscar Monet.

INTERNSHIPS

Awarded a fully paid internship in a children's art class at the Art Institute — Summer 2005

EDUCATION

School Name and Address

to success.

your road

TO CREATE

for others

Don't wait

Marcus Street, age 17

1234 Westchester Ave., Apt. 3C
Washington Station, Connecticut 45367
Phone: 834.540.0111
E-mail: marcusstreet@_____.com

CUSTOMER SERVICE LEAD AND CLERK   August 2004 to Present
Kristine's Stop & Shop: Washington Station, Connecticut — Part-time after-school position to assist my single Mom with household expenses. Replenish shelves with produce and other perishables, review product code dates to remove any expired food, price food items, assist customers in locating products, bag customers' purchases, and maintain store cleanliness.

REVENUE AND CLIENTELE GROWTH   October 2004 to Present
As a result of maintaining store cleanliness, began cleaning business owners' store windows by removing streaks, old glue, and replacing advertisement posters. Took on one new store over the past year due to the compliments received from customers and surrounding business owners, and my income has increased by 25%.

LEARNING AND DEVELOPMENT CHOICES
- Participant in church Youth Development Program — Financial management for teens: Individual Retirement Accounts (IRAs), Certificates of Deposit (CDs), stocks, bonds, investing options, mutual funds, budgeting, credit card debt management, what is a FICO Score (Fair Isaac & Company Credit-Scoring System)? Understanding your FICO Score, time management classes, and computer classes. June 2003 and June 2004
- Participant in College Bound Weekends: spent time with college students and got a taste of what college life was like. September and November 2003

GIFT PROJECT VOLUNTEER	Each Christmas Eve at our local community center, for four hours, I help distribute clothes and toys to underprivileged children. Since December 2001
COMPUTER KNOWLEDGE	FlowRinga (flowchart software), Microsoft Word, PowerPoint, Excel, Outlook Express, and Windows XP
ACTIVITIES	Enjoy playing tennis
EDUCATION	School Name and Address
AWARDS	Certificate of Achievement awarded after completion of Youth Development Program

Do things the "Write" way!

Angeline Reitmoure, age 14

READING LEVELS RAISED
Enjoy tutoring neighborhood children in reading; meet with two students for one hour twice a week. The children now read two grade levels above their own. August 2004 to Present

CONTRIBUTING WRITER — School newspaper
Most recent article tells of students' awards, graduating seniors, and colleges that accepted them. Created a column titled **Student Spotlight** which tells about different students, where they are from, what activities they enjoy, and their aspiring goals. Use web and library resources to research information for news articles, and write sidebars and captions. September 2004 to Present

ADDITIONAL STUDIES — Web site design and desktop publishing

CHILDREN'S BOOK CLUB ORGANIZER AND PRESIDENT — The Roaring Readers
Review books for future reading, sponsor in-home meetings to hold discussions of books read, and submit book reviews to neighborhood newsletter for a column titled **A Child's Perspective**.
January 2003 to Present

SPOKEN WORD EVENT ORGANIZER
Twice a year, children from the neighborhood get a chance to hold the attention of parents, grandparents, and guests as the children read interesting stories and poetry they have written. I send e-mail notifications of dates and times of events, register participants, create nametags, and am Mistress of Ceremonies. Over the past two years the number of participants has doubled.

Results: Parents comment on how this event has sparked an increase in reading for their children and decreased television time. They say trips to the library are more frequent. January 2003 to Present

DOUBLED BOOK INVENTORY
Serve as Community Liaison and enjoy collecting gently read books from neighborhood children which are donated to local hospital. Hospital administrator said that their inventory of books for the children's library has doubled. September 2002 to Present

YOUNG WRITERS' CAMP: Houston, Texas — August 2001: Activities and workshops covered:
- Building tension and suspense in a story
- Writings by different authors
- How to select a topic
- How to structure a plot
- Writing exercises with peer evaluations
- How to write a magazine feature
- Writing fiction, essays, and poetry

COMPUTER KNOWLEDGE	Microsoft Publisher, Enchantment (web site design software), Microsoft Word, PowerPoint, Excel, Outlook, Windows XP, Mac OS9, and Mac OSX
EDUCATION	School Name and Address
AWARDS	Literary Student of the Year — October 2005

124 Hightower Ave.
Liberty Village, Texas 89111

Phone: 238.401.0111
E-mail: angiesnotes@_____.com

A Caring Heart

SAMPLE RESUME — Caregiver (Babysitter) and Pet Care

Lydia Trust, age 15   819 Creekville Place
Phone: 311.222.0333   Lochmere, Washington 14767
E-mail: Acaringheart@_____.com

PET CARE — November 2004 to Present
Provide care for neighborhood families' pets while the families are away on vacation or for a weekend get-away. Learned to care for dogs, in particular, while a volunteer at the Poodle Porch.

VOLUNTEER — June to September 2004
The Poodle Porch: Lochmere, Washington — learned to properly bathe and groom different dogs and cats. Trimmed and brushed the animals' coats, clipped their nails, and replaced their chew toys. Also kept cages cleaned and deodorized. Summer position of 20 hours per week.

CAREGIVER — January 2004 to Present
Provide care for neighborhood children while parents spend an evening out. I make sure the children's chores and homework are done. I also lay out clothes for the next school day if needed.
Found that reading to young children allows for a more relaxed atmosphere before bedtime.

ANIMAL CARE PROGRAM PARTICIPANT — Camp Sumners: Ada, Washington — June 2003
This gave me hands-on experience caring for a variety of animals such as dogs, cats, rabbits, cows, horses, and more. For different animals' care, looked at surrounding noise levels, space accommodations, indoor lighting, ventilation, and more.

CLIENTELE AND REVENUE GROWTH — Advertised sitting services in subdivision directory; this increased my clientele within my subdivision and from surrounding subdivisions as well.
I obtained trusted references and an income increase of 30%.

SAFE SITTER COURSE FOR YOUTH — "Be aware before you provide care." — November 2003
I learned about:
- Dangers of loose clothing
- Emergency Contacts
- First Aid
- Glass door and window safety
- Household chemical safety
- Knowing location of all exits
- Pool safety
- Stairway safety
- Toy safety

I provide parents with a Meals & Activity Report at the end of my assignments; this outlines the child's or children's times of meals and snacks, nap times, and activities.

CERTIFICATIONS	Child and Adult Cardiopulmonary Resuscitation (CPR)
ACTIVITIES	Power Walking
HOBBIES	Learning web site design
SOFTWARE AND OPERATING SYSTEMS	Microsoft Word, Excel, PowerPoint, Access, Outlook, Enchantment (web site design software), Windows XP, and Windows 2000
EDUCATION	School Name and Address
HONOR ROLL STUDENT	Have maintained honor roll status for years 2002, 2003, and 2004.

Melodies of the Heart

are Not necessarily FOR you.

Michael Noteworthy, age 14

VIOLINIST
Have played the violin since I was six years old. Since 2001 have performed at state and citywide concerts, festivals, and fairs and had repeat performances at the downtown playhouse. Invited as youth musician to perform with the prestigious Northern Lights Orchestra.

INVITATIONS
Had the honor of playing at the White House for a Christmas gala along with other youth musicians from around the country. December 2004
My busiest times are the holidays where performances include galas at the Governor's Mansion and state and city events.

ACCOMPLISHMENTS
- For three years in a row competed for and won the position of Concertmaster's Chair at the annual citywide May Festival — 2003, 2004, and 2005
- Composed, arranged, and played two pieces for citywide festivals — 2004
- Won statewide Young Musicians Competition which is held every two years — 2004
- Auditioned and participated in the National Children's Orchestra in New York City — 2005
- Assist high school arts director in coordinating the music for theatrical events, musicals, and music symposiums — 2005 to Present
- Received the New York Certificate of Merit
- Was selected for the Governor's Honors Program in Music in 2002

HONOR ROLL STUDENT	Have maintained honor roll status all of my school years.
MEDIA APPEARANCES	Performed on local children's television network as the Featured Musician of the Month — November 2003
ORGANIZATIONS	National Scholar Society and Gifted Children's Association
VOLUNTEER	— Enjoy playing at local area nursing homes every other month for an hour at each home. — Play at two charitable events each year. January 2001 to Present
ACTIVITIES	Playing Chess
SOFTWARE AND OPERATING SYSTEMS	Musidium (composing software), Microsoft Word, PowerPoint, Access, Excel, Outlook, Windows XP, and Windows 2000
EDUCATION	School Name and Address

981 Windover Place
Fugue Harbor, New York 10455

Phone: 254.676.0189
E-mail: michaelsstrings@_____.com

Hair Ye!   Hair Ye!

Donna Hairston, age 12

777 Grace Ave., Apt. J • Pate Village, Illinois 42477 • Phone: 424.789.0511 • E-mail: dmh@_____.com

CREATIVE STYLIST
— Cleared out a small utility room in my family's apartment and set up shop. Create own weekly allowance by braiding hair. Provide creative and unique styles for birthdays, holidays, and tired Moms.

— Purchased camera, took photos of finished styles, and made a photo album for prospective customers. Began an appointment book as well as a customer e-mail base. Appointments are scheduled on Friday evenings and weekends as not to interfere with my weekday school work. Opened a savings account with monies earned. January 2005 to Present

GOLD MEDAL WINNER
Helped lead girls' track team to a championship win. Awarded two gold medals, one in the 100-meter run and one in the long jump.
Eagle Athletic Club — April 2005

LEARNING SERIES
— Major Manners Class for Youth — etiquette training
— Financial Fitness Training — learned about savings accounts, stocks, bonds, mutual funds, Certificates of Deposit (CDs), children's custodial accounts, budgeting, and how to be a wise consumer
— Attended the opera, puppet shows, and the ballet
July and August 2004

PERSONAL DEVELOPMENT
Participant in local library learning program where I learned to use Microsoft Word, PowerPoint, Excel, Mathematical Solutions, and Outlook

Certificate of Completion — June 2003

OTHER INTERESTS
Going to museums and watching educational television

EDUCATION
School Name and Address

2005 STATE MATH LEAGUE COMPETITION WINNER
Math-keteer: Junior Math Team member (7th and 8th grades)
For this win, our school team was featured on The Education Avenue television program. We discussed our winning strategy and each of us was awarded a plaque.

Tools OF THE Trade

SAMPLE RESUME — Craftsman

Victor Oni, age 17   788 Woodlawn Ave.
Phone: 234.010.0110   Landstown, Nevada 02987
E-mail: Victorstoolbelt@_____.com

EDUCATION

School Name and Address

TRAINING AND DEVELOPMENT

On some Saturdays my Dad and I attend free workshops on home improvement areas such as replacing a toilet or a sink, installing bookshelves, or grouting and caulking, etc. In our own home we replaced master bathroom hardware, caulked bathroom tubs, and pulled up old carpet, and I assisted in laying hardwood flooring in master bedroom. January 2004 to Present

COMMUNITY SERVICE

Volunteer — Housing America construction projects — Summers of 2004 and 2005
Participated in Summer Blitz where, as a team member, I helped build a house in less than a month.

SKILLED CRAFTSMAN-IN-TRAINING

Learning the lessons of home repairs and improvements from my Dad: replace cabinets, hardware on cabinets, remove wallpaper, paint, lay tile, lay hardwood floors, pavers, and replace sinks. January 2003 to Present

STUDENT EXCHANGE PROGRAM

For eight weeks, lived with a family and attended school in Barcelona, Spain. Enjoyed seeing the architecture and old monuments. On weekends spent time touring countrysides and visiting small shops. October through November 2003

COMPUTER SOFTWARE AND OPERATING SYSTEMS

Computer Aided Drafting (CAD), Microsoft Word, PowerPoint, Windows XP, HomeDesign (architecture design software), and Luxuryscapes (landscape design software)

ACCOMPLISHMENTS AND AWARDS

Won high school design competition — 1st Place award of $15,000 toward college — May 2004
I used CAD to design a mini storage system. An electrical parts company chose my design and built fifteen systems that provided the company with additional storage space in their warehouse.

HOBBIES AND ACTIVITIES

Reading home improvement magazines, watching home improvement programs, and baseball

After graduation will pursue a degree in Architecture with a minor in Construction Management.

CARPENTRY TOOLS

Basin Wrench	Hack Saw	Jigsaw	Orbital Sander
Circular Saw	Hand Plane	Level	Stud Finder
Crescent Wrench	Hand Saw	Mitersaw	Tubing Cutters

LANGUAGES — Fluent in Spanish

Paper Money

SAMPLE RESUME — Origami — Hobby turned into income

Wendy Milsap, age 10
888 Steele Ave. • Pulptown, North Dakota 98765
E-mail: WOrigami@_____.com • Phone: 777.000.8888

___

EDUCATION

School Name and Address

SUCCESSFUL CREATIVE SALES

Took my hobby, Origami, and created an income. I make decorative boxes, bags, table decorations, twist-outs, cut-a-ways, and pop-ups for my family. Decided to display my creations at an art exhibit at school; this was a big hit. Began to receive orders from parents for birthday decorations. The most requested item is the twist-out of children's names. Also put together a catalog of products that my Dad put on the Internet. He created a web page from the free web space given by our internet service provider. Since January 2003

Hosted in-home Origami show that drew 12 families from my neighborhood and school. May 2004

THEATER ASSISTANT

Was asked by the director of our school drama department to assist in producing table props, hats, and stage decorations for plays and other events. March 2003 to Present

CREATIVE EXPOSURE AND SALES AVENUE

Set up booth at local annual Children's Fall Festival where I display and sell my creations. Every October since 2003

CHARITABLE DONATIONS

Created large collection of holiday hats and presented them to local children's hospital. Create new hats to replace torn ones.

TRAINING

Learned Origami from manuals bought at local bookstores; also found how-to videos extremely helpful.

ADVENTURES IN DIVERSITY

Youth Diversity Workshop — June 2004
Lessons and activities included:

- What is diversity?
- The value of diversity
- Valuing self and others
- What creates prejudice? — a look into attitudes

- Don't miss out on friendships because people come in different "packages"
- Culture Shock — what have you heard about different cultures?
- Changing your behavior to include others

COMPUTER KNOWLEDGE

Microsoft Word, PowerPoint, Excel, and Outlook

ACTIVITIES

Tip Toe Dance Conservatory: Dance Team — Classical Ballet

You always KNOW MORE

THAN *you* think You Do.

SAMPLE RESUME — <u>No experience</u> (so he says)

Jonathan Neumoor, age 14
878 Brilliant Way • Vistaville, Georgia 77711 • Phone: 432.010.1001 • E-mail: jneumoor@ _____.com

---

EDUCATION
School Name and Address

COLLABORATION, SALES, AND INCREASED REVENUE
Work with team member in lawn care servicing, trash removal, and monthly detailing of vehicle. Joint venture in cleaning, running errands, and acquiring goods. Work with team member to establish budgets for investments, expenditures, and internal and external programs. Assist team member with increasing income through resale of perishables (candy), pre-owned video games, and providing lawn care to neighbors.

Results: Lowered amount of weekly allotment received from team member (single Mom), able to invest in a savings account, reduced entertainment costs by participating in internal programs (movie rentals for home viewing), played on church football team, and received MVP (Most Valuable Player) Award (external program).

TUTOR
Every other week for two hours I teach basic computer skills to senior citizens in our neighborhood. I show them how to send / receive e-mail, create and save documents, create file folders, insert images into documents, and more. We take turns meeting in one of their homes.   September 2005 to Present

Results:
- Friendships have been made.
- Recipes are shared after some of the sessions (my Mom and I enjoy this benefit).
- Once a month a family member of one of my students pays me for the result of my time and efforts. Half of the earnings go into my savings account.

HONOR ROLL STUDENT
Have maintained a minimum 3.8 Grade Point Average (GPA) for two years in a row.

TRAINING
Self-taught: Microsoft PowerPoint, and continue training through use of school computers.

COMPUTER SKILLS
Microsoft Word, PowerPoint, Access, Excel, Outlook

ACTIVITIES
Participated in Summer football camp (2005), enjoy playing basketball, and video games.

And the Next Book is?

Abigail Reading, age 12
665 Hope Terrace, Apt. A • Textown, Alaska 67653
E-mail: abbysbooknook@_____.com • Phone: 834.812.3110

EDUCATION
School Name and Address

GOVERNMENT CLASSES — Summer 2005
- United States Presidents
- The Making of Laws
- Running for Congressional Office
- The Declaration of Independence
- The Presidential Election Process

WASHINGTON SCHOLAR
As a result of my community involvement, was chosen to attend the Washington Scholars Public Policy, Science and Technology (PPST) Program held in Washington, DC. Interacted with members of Congress, lobbyists, presidential appointees, journalists, and other officials. Visited congressional offices as well as other national sites. September 2005

ENCOURAGE READING AT AN EARLY AGE
Serve as a Young Reader for local library. For 45 minutes two days a week I read to four-year olds. The Young Reader Program began in 2003 and has more than doubled its participants. My class alone has 8 to 10 children at each reading session. September 2003 to Present

REVIEWER
Along with other Young Readers, review books one month in advance for upcoming reading sessions. Make and post flyers on library community bulletin board outlining reading session dates, times, locations, and cancellations. September 2003 to Present

SPANISH BOOK CLUB FOUNDER
Have been taking Spanish in school since 2001 and in 2003 formed a Spanish book club and put together a suggested reading list of Spanish authors. Our Spanish book club now reads a minimum of three books a year from this list.

AWARDS
Presented with the 2004 Community Service Award for Youth — given by the state of Alaska <u>Recipients of the award have significantly contributed to humanities, education, science, the arts, family, public policy, or other areas, in a way that benefits the development of gifts and talents in young people.</u>

NEWSPAPER FEATURE
Featured in local newspaper for being among 25 students chosen to go to Washington, DC for the PPST Program and for the Community Service Award.

COMPUTER SOFTWARE AND SKILLS
SpectroWord (encyclopedia), Microsoft Word, Excel, Outlook, Lotus Notes, and the Internet

A Few simple Steps Can Carry you and others a Long way.

Deborah Abel, age 8
555 Ability Ave. • Coastaltown, Maine 00000
Phone: 876.321.2345 • E-mail: healthykids@_____.com

EDUCATION School Name and Address

CHILDREN'S WALK FOR WELLNESS FOUNDER — As a result of struggling with my own weight began walking with my Mom in our neighborhood. Looked for children in the neighborhood who wanted to walk with us. I did this by making flyers that explained:

- Reason for **Children's Walk for Wellness**
- Days, hours, and how long walks would be
- Goals

Results:
- Have over 25 children and parents walking on Saturday mornings and two evenings a week. Children and parents from surrounding neighborhoods have joined us.
- Parents get together and exchange healthy recipes that children will like.
- <u>Biggest result — seven children have lost 10 pounds or more each and have kept the weight off, and I am one of these children.</u>
- My Mom created a website, **Children's Walk for Wellness.** It encourages children from all over the world to begin their own **Children's Walk for Wellness** campaign. It has before-and-after pictures of children who have reached their goal weights. The site has stories about children and their families, a walking schedule, and healthy recipes. We give encouragement through e-mails.
Most of the time our growing group meets at a park to walk. We communicate by e-mail for updates, date changes, and cancellations. May 2004 to Present

TRI-CITY YOUTH HEALTH & WELLNESS ASSOCIATION — youngest member on council

MEDIA APPEARANCES
I gave a half hour interview on The Kids Beat (Public Broadcasting) and told how I started **Children's Walk for Wellness**, spoke about my weight struggle, and showed before-and-after pictures of myself and of other children's weight loss. I am asked to make guest appearances on kids' health shows.

SPEAKING APPEARANCES — 2004 and 2005
- Began at my own school's health fair and talked to my classmates about healthy eating habits, the importance of exercise, and shared healthy recipes – School name
- Pound Elementary, Caring Academy, and Stonington Elementary health fairs

COMPUTER SKILLS — Internet, Microsoft Word, PowerPoint, and Outlook

ACTIVITIES
Gardening with my Mom, attending puppet shows, and bike riding (I don't get out of breath anymore.)

Home is where the Heart is.

SAMPLE RESUME — "Home" Training

Daniel Cramer, age 6   888 Warren Place
                                                            Houseford, California 10203
                                                            Phone: 234.432.2005

EDUCATION   School Name and Address

QUICKIDS LEARNING — An advanced early-childhood development center. I began to read at three years old and to learn about science, math, art, and more. September 2003 to August 2005

SUMMER LEARNING SERIES 2005 — (ages 5 to 10)
Disaster Education Training
- Fire awareness — the Stop, Drop, and Roll technique
- Smoke Detector Basics — what are they?
- Playing with matches — A NO, NO!

Be ready in an emergency for house fires, storms, earthquakes, and floods
- Know where flashlights are kept
- Know the safest place in your house when a storm is coming
- What to do, what not to do, and how to get out of the house fast in case of a fire

Home Alone Video Series
- Talking to Strangers — A NO, NO!
- When to call 911
- A "Do Call" List in case of an emergency

CREATED INCOME / LEAD STUDENT / ORGANIZER
- Help my Dad keep the family car presentable (washing it), rake leaves in front and backyards, gather household trash for weekly pickup, and do other chores as given by parents.
- Help with the care of my younger brother and sister (two-year old twins) by straightening our family room after playtime.
- I set aside half an hour every Monday and Wednesday evenings to read to my parents. They read to us children on Friday and Saturday evenings.
Results:
— Mom and Dad spend less time picking up (or stepping on) toys after we have gone to bed.
— For helping to care for my brother and sister, Mom and Dad —on a monthly basis— happily put more money in my savings.

WALK-A-THON VOLUNTEER — To benefit a local children's hospital, I raised $360.00 for cancer and childhood disease research (I spent most of the walk on my Dad's shoulders). June 2005
THE LANGUAGE LOFT: Raya, California — Began learning to speak German. January 2004
ACTIVITIES — Soccer and playing Chinese Checkers
COMPUTER SKILLS — Math and language software as well as Microsoft Word, Internet, and computer games
ORGANIZATIONS — Gifted Children's Association

InVentor's Dream

Mark Bourne, age 12
878 Wisteria Lane. • SageTown, Oregon 96812
E-mail: patentthis@_____.com • Phone: 770.310.0700

EDUCATION	School Name and Address
PATENTS	Granted a patent in 2003 for a new children's game.
ORGANIZATIONS	The National Association for Young Inventors — 2004 Inductee

COMPUTER CAMP — SmarTech Inc., Sage Town, Oregon — June 2005
I Learned C++ programming and JAVA. Put my new-found skills to work and programmed motors, gears, and switches. I designed and built my own robot and applied my skills to a new robotic design system. The basic and advance programming classes were challenging and fun.

YOUTH SUMMER ENRICHMENT PROGRAM — June 2004
Took courses in:
- Advanced Math
- Computer Courses: Microsoft Word, Excel, PowerPoint, Access, and Outlook
- Creative Writing
- Reading
- Social Skills and Etiquette

TEACHING SUCCESSFULLY — Enjoy sitting down twice a week for one hour with two neighborhood children and teaching math basics. Found really cool math web sites to assist the children.

Results: Their parents have seen a rise in their children's math test scores. September 2003 to Present

VOLUNTEER — September 2003 to Present
Before volunteering was required to participate in a relationships workshop, A Caring Heart.
This program is for youth who interact with senior citizens.
Learned:
- Overview of the Aging Process
- How to respond to the needs of older adults

Taking Care of Our Own Team: We have several senior citizens in the neighborhood that need grass cut and leaves raked. Some of us wash their vehicles when needed. Other kids and I take turns visiting individuals and reading to them. I put together a list of phone numbers of our team members so if any of our seniors need assistance they may call us.

THE LANGUAGE HUT — June 2000 to Present
Joined a children's language group where I began to learn Portuguese. I now communicate with my grandmother who is from Brazil.

HONOR ROLL STUDENT
Have maintained honor roll status for two years in a row.

ACTIVITIES Playing lacrosse and learning computer programming

Hearing for someone
else Can Benefit both of You.

SAMPLE RESUME — Sign Language Interpreter

Dakota Shaw, age 13

353 Audible Ave.
Cambridge, Oklahoma 00000
Phone: 334.010.0452
E-mail: dakotashands@_____.com

___

INTERPRETER — When I was seven I began learning sign language because my best friend is deaf. My Mom bought books on learning to sign. I took sign language classes and now I am an interpreter in children's church. As the Sunday school teacher reads the lesson, I sign for children who are hearing-impaired. Other children are beginning to learn sign language so they too can become interpreters for our Sunday school classes.

Results: An increase in the number of hearing-impaired children in our Sunday school classes. Parents comment that they appreciate interpreters for their children and not just for the adults. January 2003 to Present

NOTE: Modes of signing — SEE (Signing Exact English) and ASL (American Sign Language)

SUMMER STUDIES — June 2005
Corraven College: Raine, Oklahoma — Skills Recognition Program (SRP) which encourages elementary and high school students to learn more about the skills they have as they identify their talents and abilities.

Classes taken:
- Know Who You Are and Identify Your Capabilities
- Creative Thought
- Humanities
- Speed Reading and Comprehension
- Writing

YOUNG VOICE PUBLIC SPEAKING PROGRAM — July 2004
Because I stutter, I decided to participate in this program to boost my confidence when speaking to a group.
- Active Listening
- Effective Movement and Gestures
- Fundamentals of Public Speaking
- Know Your Audience
- Preparing and Practicing Speaking
- Selecting a Topic
- Speaking to Inform
- Speaking to Persuade
- Speech Planning and Writing
- Speech Tips
- Visual Aids

THE READER'S CIRCLE ORGANIZER — June 2003 to Present
Organized a group of children who have speech challenges (lisp, stutter, mispronunciation of letters, etc.). We meet at different homes once a week for two hours, sit in a circle, and read aloud to one another. Some of the children have seen improvement in their speech.

AWARDS	Young Scholar, Corraven College: Raine, Oklahoma — Skills Recognition Program
HOBBY	Collecting and watching old cartoons on Digital Video Discs (DVDs) such as Charlie Brown, Bugs Bunny, Felix the Cat, Mighty Mouse, and Woody Woodpecker.
ACTIVITES	Ultimate Frisbee and Volleyball
COMPUTER SOFTWARE	Microsoft Word, Excel, PowerPoint, Outlook
EDUCATION	School Name and Address

BANK on It!

SAMPLE RESUME — Saver / Investor

Christine Banks, age 14
373 Currency Lane • Mormonny, New Jersey 45798
E-mail: CJBanks33@_____.com • Phone: 334.010.0088

EDUCATION School Name and Address (International Studies / Baccalaureate Program)

GENERATED FUNDS AND INCREASED FINANCIAL PORTFOLIO
At a very young age began saving spare change received from my parents, grandparents, and friends. Saved approximately $475.00 in one year from collecting change, then used it to open a Y.A.P. Account (Young Adults Plus). Every month I deposit a set amount of my allowance into this account. The two custodial accounts opened by my parents and grandparents have seen significant growth the past three years.

YOUTH SUMMER ENRICHMENT PROGRAM — Investment Camp — Summers 2003 and 2004
Learned about investing through the stock market. This was a five-week program that included:

- Introduction to Investment Terminology
- Trading Concepts
- Stock Performance Measures
- Stock Charting and Stock Indicators
- Hands-on trading with simulated money
- A free set-up of a live brokerage account at the end of the course

- Budgeting
- Introduction to Mutual Funds
- Individual Retirement Accounts: (Roth and Traditional)
- Money Management

ORGANIZATIONS
National Association of Young Investors — Member since 2003 (at age 12 joined an investment club)

CLUB COORDINATOR
Began a monthly Kids Money Management Club in my neighborhood. We meet in our clubhouse to discuss ways to earn income, ways of investing, share investing literature, and explore investing web sites; some web sites have financial games for us to play. January 2003 to Present

READING MATERIALS
IY (Investing Young) Magazine
Young Business Minded Magazine (for teen entrepreneurs)
Money Management for Teens

COMPUTER SKILLS — Vitalectra (financial software), QuickBooks, Microsoft Word, and Access

CHILDLIKE, INC. YOUTH VOLUNTEER — One Saturday for two hours every other month assist in sorting, by size, donated and gently worn children's clothing. Since September 2001

YOUNG CHEFS OF AMERICA INC., Lee, New Jersey — I take cooking classes which cover kitchen safety, setting a table, proper food handling, proper use of food thermometers, and more. I love learning to cook gourmet from watching TV shows. For the past three Christmases I've treated myself to gourmet cookbooks. January 2001 to Present

GOAL — I plan to become an Investment Banker.

Healing Hands

SAMPLE RESUME — <u>Aspiring Medical Professional</u>

Anna Wellspring, age 15   975 Rock Cove Ave., Apt. 7D
Phone: 770.922.3001   Hanover, North Carolina 89612
                                                          E-mail: Awellspring@_____.com

I would like to pursue a career in Medical Research. Individuals are living longer, and
I believe in renewed health in order to enjoy that longer life span.

RESEARCH FELLOW: Summer 2005
High school summer science research fellowship program, Ocean State University. Participated in a gene discovery research project that resulted in significant information concerning various cancers. Learned how to formulate and test hypotheses, conducted experiments, collected data, and assisted scientist by participating in analyses. Wrote and submitted a scientific paper on my research project, then entered my project in a science competition where I was awarded second place. Attended seminars and lectures each week; especially enjoyed the question and answer sessions. At the end of the program other fellows and I presented our research projects to our mentors, lab team members, families, and friends.

LABORATORY EXPERIENCE:
Conducted experiments in cell culture lab with science faculty mentors and grew overnight cultures. Assisted in research projects that addressed the causes, prevention, and treatment for heart disease. Prepared solutions and media, aseptic sampling, dilutions, cleaned and set up lab equipment, organized sample rooms, and calibrated thermometers.

TRAINING AND DEVELOPMENT: Summer 2004
Youth Medical Symposium participant — A program for high school students who demonstrate academic excellence and are interested in a medical career. Topics included ethics in medicine, public policy and health, and medical research options. Was also given a fictitious "patient" for whom I learned to diagnose and develop a treatment plan. Visited several hospitals and laboratories and spent time with physicians, researchers, scientists, nurses, interns, and hospital administrators.

FOUNDER: School Medi-Squad — A 15-member team of CPR-certified students.
At least two students are present at the school's sporting events in case of an emergency — Begun May 2004

CERTIFICATIONS:
Child and Adult CPR (Cardiopulmonary Resuscitation) / Automated External Defibrillator (AED)

VOLUNTEER: Happy Hands Shelter: serve meals to families, distribute job information, assist in setting up medical screening areas, and distribute toiletries one Saturday every month for four hours. 2003 to Present

COMPUTER SKILLS: Bacertrak (data analysis & retrieval software), Ubiquitrace (statistical analysis software), Microlyst (data management software), Microsoft Word, Excel, Access, and PowerPoint

ACTIVITIES: I enjoy opera. My grandparents buy season tickets to attend productions they like. I happen to enjoy the operas they don't like, so I get to go to Atlanta (with adult family member) and attend at least three times a year.

EDUCATION: School Name and Address

homeSchooled

Nicholas Daniels, age 11
377 Booker Rd. • Safe Haven, Wisconsin 11123
E-mail: homestead377@_____.com • Phone: 884.010.0147

EDUCATION
Nordic Homeschooling Association

YOUNG WRITER'S AWARD WINNER – March 2005
Awarded First Place – Essay: The World in the Year 2050. I imagined what the world would be like: how we would live, where we would live, and what foods would be here for us to eat.

2004 SPELLING BEE FINALIST
Was one of ten finalists in State Spelling Bee

TEAM BUILDING TRAINING – August 2004
Other children in my homeschooling group and I took the following classes:
- Active Listening
- Effective Relationships
- Creating Calm Surroundings
- Nurturing Your Teammates
- Trusting
- The Mystery
- Role Playing

ORGANIZED SHAREWARE PROGRAM
Created and implemented a **ShareWare** program where homeschooling families within our group can rotate / share educational software. This system is like a library where families can check out software, use it for a certain length of time, and then return it. Began program September 2003.

ASPIRING AUTHOR
Since I was seven, I have been writing down each year of homeschooling experiences, activities, and lessons, and writing a book for children who are starting to be homeschooled. These children will get a first-hand account, from another homeschooled child, of what to expect during their years of home-schooling. Book Title: The Homeschooled Experience – A Child's Perspective.

ACTIVITIES
- Crescent County Soccer League: I play Forward on my team, The Swift Kickers — play in the Fall
- Safe Haven Gymnastics Club — enjoy the parallel bars and the rings — year round program

COMPUTER KNOWLEDGE
Microsoft Publisher, Word, Excel, PowerPoint, Outlook, and Mathematical Solutions

Scoop Newsworthy

SAMPLE RESUME — Aspiring Radio Broadcaster

Aaron Whittington, age 15

975 SoundView Blvd., Apt. 4F
Neward, Kansas 59612
E-mail: aaronontheair@_____.com
Phone: 770.822.3001

SUMMER RADIO SYMPOSIUM — August 2003
This is a two-week program for students whose interests are in radio broadcasting. I mingled and networked with radio personalities and took the following workshops:
- Broadcast Ethics
- Broadcast Law and how to research topics
- Commercial Production and Announcing
- Journalism Basics
- Producing Programs and Formatting
- Radio Broadcasting Equipment Basics
- Sports Announcing

RADIO BROADCASTER — September 2004 to Present
I am part of a team that runs our high school radio station, WDKM 88.7 AM.
I created the school's only talk show called **You Talk, We Listen** that airs community affairs and schoolers' thoughts.

- Am learning broadcast engineering and rules, policies, and procedures in retaining a broadcasting license.
- Successfully put together program formats.

HOBBIES
- Since I was seven years old have been "hamming" it up on the radio with my uncle who is a Licensed Amateur (Ham) Radio Operator. We talk to people in surrounding communities, states, and around the world.
- Am learning Internet Broadcasting and about Podcasting.

THE YOUNG BROADCASTER'S VOICE AWARD WINNER — October 2005
I was presented this award by my school for creative broadcasting.

VOLUNTEER — Enjoy sharing about being a radio broadcaster at Children Going Places. This is a statewide program that encourages youth to get involved with various events, programs, training, volunteer work, and other areas that will help them uncover and grow their talents, skills, and abilities. January 2005 to Present

COMPUTER SKILLS — RadioFlare (broadcasting software), Microsoft Word, Excel, Access, PowerPoint, and Outlook

ACTIVITIES — Indoor soccer

EDUCATION — School Name and Address

Swim for your life

Adam S. Tamura, age 15
Phone: 384.010.0147
Fax: 384.010.1147

397 Waterford Lane
Lancaster, Florida 10123
E-mail: astamura@_____.com

EDUCATION: School Name and Address

VOLUNTEER: Fish store called the Exotic Aquarium — June and August 2005
The owner taught classes on all the shop's slippery inhabitants. I learned different types of marine life and how to care for different types of coral, sponges, and clams.

SCUBA (**S**elf **C**ontained **U**nderwater **B**reathing **A**pparatus) **Certification**: **Open Water Diver.** July 2005

BIOLOGY RESEARCH CAMP: Underwater Investigations Inc., Lancaster, Florida — June 2004
- Program included ecology and aquatic studies with that of microbiology and molecular biology.
- Took water samples from a lake and analyzed water quality and the possible effects it can have on aquatic life.
- Tested levels of pH and chemicals in water samples.
- Learned to identify plankton.
- Plated "friendly" bacteria samples and visited research labs.

SEA CAMP: Sea Ya! Inc., Camia, Florida — June 2003: Snorkeled in the coral reef and took classes:
- Coral Ecology
- Dune and Beach Ecology
- Estuarine Ecology
- Marine Botany
- Marine Geology
- Marine Vertebrates and Invertebrates
- Oceanography Principles
- Plankton Communities / Plankton Lab

GEAR / EQUIPMENT USED AND OPERATED

Bottom Dredges	Pipettes	Sample Tubes
Fishing Nets	Plankton Nets	Water Quality Test Kits
Microscope	Refractometer	Water Sampling Bottles

Introduced to underwater photography and took pictures of different marine life. Was taught water safety and how to recognize and stay away from hazardous water conditions.

JR. SEA CAMP: Sea Ya! Inc., Camia, Florida — June 2001 (**Belize**). Program included:
- Kayaking
- Marine Biology Basics
- Marine Lab
- Rock Wall Climbing
- Sailing
- SCUBA Terminology
- Snorkeling (Dive Equipment Basics / Assembly)

YOUTH CONSERVATION CAMP: Earthy Inc., Allpy, California — July 2000. Program covered:
- Concepts of Ecology
- Boating Safety
- Discussion on predator / prey relationships
- Endangered species
- Fish Netting
- Identification of fish species
- Protecting the habitat
- Skills necessary to live outdoors

- continued -

CAREER DAY SPEAKER — Visit elementary and high schools and share about being a youth diver. Bring in diving equipment and show a movie about marine life. September 2005 to Present

CERTIFICATIONS	— Adult and Child CPR (Cardiopulmonary Resuscitation) / Automated External Defibrillator (AED)
HOBBIES	Rowing and I have my own 30-gallon synthetic coral reef aquarium at home
COMPUTER KNOWLEDGE	Microlyst (data management software), Windows XP, Windows 2000, Microsoft Word, Excel, and PowerPoint
ORGANIZATIONS	National Scholar Society and Florida Youth Aquatics Club (ages 12 to 17)

Sample References

School

Ms. Casey Westmoreland, Counselor
Howe Elementary School
1855 Haggarty Ave.
Seabring, NY 11437
718.964.0000

Mrs. Leah Morgan, Teacher (6th and 7th grades)
Chancellor Academy
452 Royer Rd.
Seabring, NY 11435
718.908.3210

Mr. Paul Flemming, Teacher (Calculus)
Reisling Montessori School
1911 Spring St., SE
Seabring, NY 11436
718.911.2236

Athletics

Ms. Lisa Cunningham, Girls Softball Coach
Raine Athletics, Inc.
956 Chloe Ave.
Seabring, NY 11435
718.596.2211, Extension 102

Mr. Jonathan Nichols, Boys Baseball Coach
Remmington High School
975 Lisbon Rd.
Seabring, NY 11437
718.678.4212

Clergy

Michael Wright, Youth Pastor
Lighthouse Ministries of Seabring
352 Light Trail
Seabring, NY 11435
718.351.2236

Community Service

Ms. Tabitha Sims - Volunteer Services
Mercy Medical Center
928 West Way
Seabring, NY 11437
718.862.3200, Extension 352

Family Friends

The Colemans
Lou & Peg Coleman
Lisa and Andrew (children)
771 Alpine Way
Seabring, NY 11437
718.579.5200

The Scotts
Mac & Rachel Scott
Keith, Luke, and Sophia (children)
412 Heath Lane
Seabring, NY 11435
718.357.4122

SAMPLE COVER LETTER   *Both student and parent(s) are to sign cover letter.

Overseas Experience

Mr. and Mrs. John Mays
Parents of Julie Mays
964 River Rd.
Hudson Place, MD 97832

January 15, 2006

Mr. and Mrs. Michael Ramsey
495 Jolly Way, SE
Hudson Place, MD 97934

Hello Mr. and Mrs. Ramsey:

I have been attending a summer language learning and volunteer program and studying French for the past seven years. To continue with my studies and volunteer service my school, Richland Hills Academy, is offering a trip to Paris, France where a portion of our time will be spent cleaning and restoring parks and other recreational facilities and a portion will be spent in the classroom. The overseas experience will mirror the summer program.

Please review my resume and program information which serve as an invitation for you to participate in my growth and development. As you can see from my resume my activities are in line with the program offerings. My heart is to be part of an organization that serves the needs of the poor around the world, and this program will help me reach that goal, but this opportunity will cost me something else — dollars and cents.

I am looking for financial assistance to participate in this program and you are one of twenty sponsors we are asking to give $50.00. We are looking for one-half of the finances to come from generous sponsors like you. Several corporations have already provided one-half of the funding. As a sponsor you will receive a letter of appreciation and your name will appear on the sponsorship page of my school's web site. The deadline for all finances to be received by my school is March 15th. All checks and money orders should be made payable to Richland Hills Academy with my full name on the "For" line at the bottom of the check or money order. My parents have enclosed a self-addressed stamped envelope for your convenience. Thank you so very much for taking the time to read this and for your participation.

Sincerely,

Julie Mays, age 13 (student)

Mr. and Mrs. John Mays (parents)

SAMPLE COVER LETTER   *Both student and parent(s) are to sign cover letter.

Camp Participant

Ms. Rachel Long
Parent of Michael Long   2236 Alpine Trail • Atlanta, GA 30321

January 15, 2006

Ms. Nancy Moss
778 Heritage Way
Conyers, GA 30014

Hello Ms. Moss:

This letter, my resume, and program information serve as your invitation to have a part in my growth and development. The Leaps and Bounds Association gives partial sponsorship to students from schools throughout the state to attend Math and Computer Camp and I have been chosen by my school to attend camp this summer. Through this program I will continue to learn advanced algebra, geometry, and other math concepts. I will learn more of the Microsoft Office Suite of software and have access to other teaching software as well.

There is a cost and that is where I am looking for full sponsorship to participate in the program. You are one of ten sponsors we are asking to give $50.00. If you have not already, please take some time to review the camp information. If you look at the activities on my resume you will see that they line up with the activities offered in the camp. I have enjoyed participating in these types of programs for the past three years and they have prepared me to do well academically.

Checks and money orders are to be made payable to The Leaps and Bounds Association with my name and program name on the bottom of the check or money order. My Mom has enclosed a self-addressed stamped envelope for you. The deadline for finances to be received by the Association is May 15th. At the end of camp I will receive a certificate of completion and the certificate will display the names of my sponsors. All sponsors will receive a recognition letter from The Leaps and Bounds Association. Thank you for taking the time to read this and for your generosity.

Sincerely,

Michael Long (student)

Ms. Rachel Long (parent)

SAMPLE COVER LETTER

Competition Applicant

January 15, 2006

Ms. Cecelia Mitchell
Legal Guardian of Aaron Michaels
6400 Colgate Dr., Apt. 3-C
Lovejoy, CA 92577

Mr. and Mrs. Louis Richardson
898 Vista Park Dr.
Shelby, IL 21497

Hello Mr. and Mrs. Richardson:

A wonderful opportunity has come my way in the form of a state artists' competition. To enter I was required to submit a portfolio of my work — pencil drawings and water color drawings. Participants were chosen based on the acceptance of the portfolio. Now I have three months to send in the registration fee of $500.00. We are looking for full sponsorship with all checks and money orders made payable to The Art for Kids Foundation with my name and 2006 Arts Competition on the bottom of the check or money order. The $500.00 registration fee covers the following:

- Entrance into the competition
- Booth space to display my work
- Free display space for six months in three local art galleries
- Name, picture, and two of my drawings in the 2006 Children's Who's Who in the World of Art Catalogue

Please review my resume and the Foundation's program information. You will see that your generous giving will have a great part in my growth and development in this area that I love so much, and you are one of ten sponsors we are asking for $50.00. All sponsors will receive a recognition letter from The Art for Kids Foundation.

The deadline for all finances to be received by the Foundation is April 28th. A self-addressed stamped envelope is enclosed for your convenience. Thank you for your generosity and support.

Sincerely,

Aaron Michaels (student)

Ms. Cecelia Mitchell (Legal Guardian)

PEARLS OF WISDOM

Some areas to explore:

- As your child performs different tasks how do those tasks relate to their abilities, talents, accomplishments, interests, or growth?
- What were the results of those tasks?
- What did your child do to overcome any unexpected problems?
- What does your child do to benefit others?
- Add to your child's resume favorable comments or brief quotes from teachers and/or notable observers of your child's activities.
- For writers look into writing contests for youth as well as local and corporate writing competitions.
- For children who aspire to become pilots research schools that offer the curriculum and flight training.
- For aspiring graphic artists research arts classes, children's art contests, art shows, businesses that will display a child's art, and corporate art competitions. Don't forget an in-home art exhibit.
- Other resources to look into are church, community, city, county, or state summer enrichment programs, courses, and learning series. Other avenues include corporate-sponsored kids' programs and colleges and universities that have youth programs.
- For savings and investing look into summer enrichment classes. Surf the Internet for children's financial classes. Look for money magazines for children. Investigate banks and credit unions that offer accounts for children.
- To own a business look for teen entrepreneur web sites, income generating for youth, and youth entrepreneur day camps.
- To become a skilled craftsman do volunteer work, small projects around the house, read home improvement magazines, and attend free home improvement classes.
- For hobbies search web sites that give ideas for hobbies and look for how-to videos.
- Research unique summer, day, and weekend camps.
- Visit your local library and ask what children's programs it offers.
- Children can make charitable contributions.
- Your child can give a presentation to his or her classmates on the different classes available to their age groups, e.g., disaster training for elementary-school children.
- Your child can create a booklet on free or inexpensive camps for children.

- continued -

- If your child provides babysitting services encourage the child to learn sign language. This shows a caring heart and brings a high level of comfort to the parents of a hearing-impaired child that the sitter will understand their child.
- Encourage your child to learn another language.
- If your child speaks another language, or several languages, have the resume translated into those languages.
- Give your child the opportunity to study and/or vacation abroad.
- Help to develop a glocal (global and local) minded individual — your child.

Reflections

❧

Reflections

∽

Reflections

❧

Reflections

❧

Reflections

❧

Reflections

∽

Reflections

❦

Reflections

_

Reflections

❧

Reflections

Reflections

❦

Ideas

Ideas

❧

Ideas

❧

Ideas

Ideas

❧

Ideas

Ideas

❧

Ideas

Ideas

❧

Ideas

❧

Ideas

❧

Ideas

Ideas

❦

Ideas

(lined blank page)

Ideas

෯

Ideas

_____

_____

_____

_____

_____

_____

_____

_____

_____

_____

_____

_____

_____

Resources

❧

Resources

&

Resources

❧

Resources

Resources

※

Resources

❧

Resources

❦

Resources

❧

Resources

Resources

～

Resources

❦